D1404290

Grocer

by **Dana Meachen Rau**

Reading Consultant: Nanci R. Vargus, Ed.D.

Marshall Cavendish
Benchmark
New York

Picture Words

 boxes

 bread

 broom

 cans

cash register

 fruit

 grocer

 truck

3

A  works in a market.

A meets the .

Words to Know

cash register (cash REJ-is-tuhr)
   a machine that holds and adds
   up money

sweeps
   cleans up with a broom

Find Out More

Books

Doyle, Charlotte. *Supermarket!* Cambridge, MA: Candlewick Press, 2004.

Hoena, B. A. *A Visit to the Supermarket*. Minneapolis: Pebble Plus, 2004.

Reggier, DeMar. *Good Food*. Danbury, CT: Children's Press, 2006.

Videos

Salter Street Films. *Works: Fantastic Food*. Sony Wonder.

Web Sites

Kids' Health: Nutrition and Fitness Center
www.kidshealth.org/kid/stay_healthy/food/nutrition_center.html

USDA: MyPyramid.gov
www.mypyramid.gov/kids/index.html

About the Author

Dana Meachen Rau is an author, editor, and illustrator. A graduate of Trinity College in Hartford, Connecticut, she has written more than two hundred books for children, including nonfiction, biographies, early readers, and historical fiction. She goes grocery shopping with her family in Burlington, Connecticut.

About the Reading Consultant

Nanci R. Vargus, Ed.D., wants all children to enjoy reading. She used to teach first grade. Now she works at the University of Indianapolis. Nanci helps young people become teachers. She likes to grocery shop in her hometown of Indianapolis, Indiana.

Marshall Cavendish Benchmark
99 White Plains Road
Tarrytown, NY 10591-9001
www.marshallcavendish.us

All Internet addresses were correct at the time of printing.

Library of Congress Cataloging-In-Publication Data
Rau, Dana Meachen, 1971-
Grocer / by Dana Meachen Rau.
       p. cm. — (Benchmark rebus)
Includes bibliographical references.
ISBN 978-0-7614-2720-9
1. Grocers—Juvenile literature. I. Title. II. Series.

HD8039.G8R38 2007
381'.456413—dc22

        2007008724

Editor: Christine Florie
Publisher: Michelle Bisson
Art Director: Anahid Hamparian
Series Designer: Virginia Pope

Photo research by Connie Gardner

Rebus images, with the exception of broom, cash register, grocer, and truck, provided courtesy of *Dorling Kindersley.*

Cover Photo by Ariel Skelley/CORBIS

The photographs in this book are used with permission and through the courtesy of:
Brigitte Sporrer/Zefa/CORBIS, p. 2 (broom); Mauritius/SuperStock, p. 3 (grocer); Prisma/SuperStock, p. 3 (truck); *Corbis*: p. 5 Layne Kennedy; p. 13 Chuck Savage; p. 21 Warren Morgan; *PhotoEdit*: pp. 7, 9 Michael Newman; pp. 17, 19 Robin Nelson; p. 11 David R. Frazier; *Alamy*: p. 15 David Hancock.

Printed in Malaysia
1 3 5 6 4 2